This story is about a real dog with a real big problem who really lived in our home when we were missionaries. His Cambodian name was Deetdoey, but for your story we thought you might find it easier to call him Jip. This special dog taught me lots about how sin is so terribly dirty, how God is so super loving, and how Jesus is so wonderfully forgiving. I hope you learn lots from him, too. Stay close to Jesus all your life! That's the safest place to be.

—Pastor Scott Griswold

TEACH Services, Inc.
P U B L I S H I N G

Copyright © 2014 Sarah E. Brown
Copyright © 2014 TEACH Services, Inc.
ISBN-13: 978-1-4796-0364-0 (Paperback)
ISBN-13: 978-1-4796-0365-7 (iBook)
ISBN-13: 978-1-4796-0366-4 (Kindle Fire)
Library of Congress Control No: 2012949838

The PRODIGAL PUP

By
SARAH E. BROWN
Illustrations by John Fraser

I0136148

I struggled, but my master held me firmly in the bathtub. Water sloshed all over the ground as I desperately tried to escape. My master poured cool water over my back, completely soaking my fur.

Next he brought out a little bottle of shampoo. As he opened the bottle, I smelled a terrible, sweet smell! My master squirted the stinky goo into my fur and began rubbing it in—worst of all, he seemed to enjoy the flowery scent! But the smell of that shampoo filled my nostrils and completely covered up the luscious aroma of the sewer slop I had just rolled in.

You probably don't understand what I'm talking about, so let me explain....

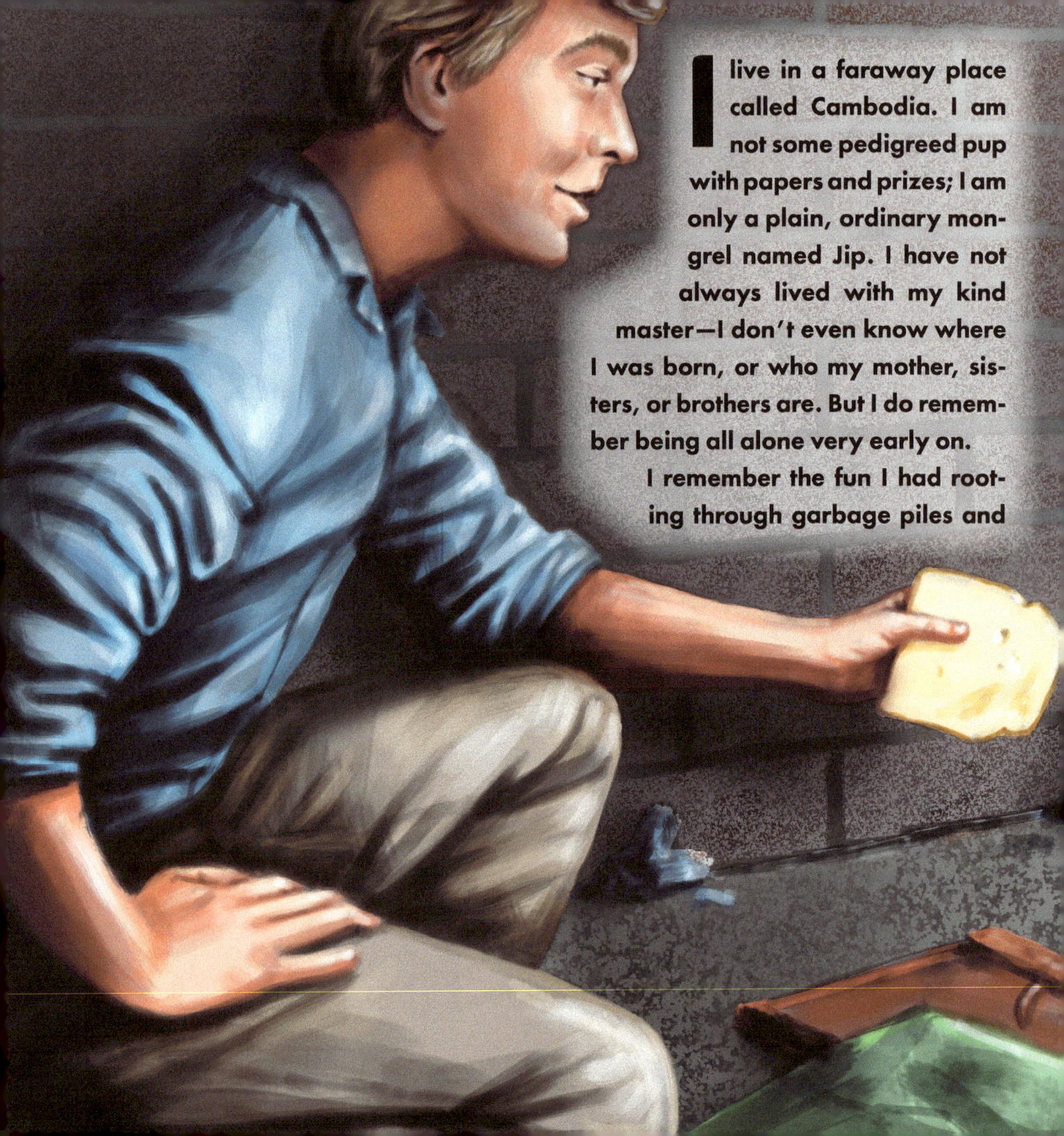

I live in a faraway place called Cambodia. I am not some pedigreed pup with papers and prizes; I am only a plain, ordinary mongrel named Jip. I have not always lived with my kind master—I don't even know where I was born, or who my mother, sisters, or brothers are. But I do remember being all alone very early on.

I remember the fun I had rooting through garbage piles and

snacking on choice scraps and tidbits that people had thrown away. But street life wasn't all fun and games. Sometimes I could hardly bear the long, lonely nights.

But my whole life changed when I met my master! He and his family had just arrived in Cambodia as missionaries. When he found me curled up in an alley, he took me home with him, and his whole family fell in love with me.

My master's daughter carefully brushed and combed my matted fur, making it soft and silky. Then his wife fed me a delicious meal. By that time I felt as good as new, and, best of all, I now had a family to love and care for me. So you can understand why I couldn't help but love such kind people as my master and his family.

Over the next few days, my new family trained me to come and sit and stay. I learned quickly and liked to please them, but I had some bad habits that were hard to get rid of. For example, I loved to roll in smelly things. It felt so good to wriggle around in the soft, cool mud to escape the hot midday sun. And after the mud dried on my fur, it shielded me from nasty bugs and the sweltering sunlight.

One of my favorite places was the large sewage puddle in my village, where I often went to roll and play. The most delicious sewer smells wafted from this puddle. Soon after my master adopted me, I went again to the puddle for my usual romp. I splashed and frolicked in the puddle all morning until every inch of my coat was covered in mud.

However, for reasons I just couldn't understand, when I went home my master was very unhappy with my looks and odor! I tried to cuddle up to him to cheer him up, but he quickly pushed me away. Then my master brought out the hated bathtub and the awful-smelling shampoo! This is where my story began.

After finishing my bath, my master set me down in front of him and looked me straight in the eye. "Now, Jip, you must stay home and not go rolling in any more smelly puddles!" He spoke kindly but firmly. So I decided I would just have to stay away from the sewer puddle from then on. After all, I wanted to please my master.

I opened my eyes the next morning at the same moment the golden rays of sunlight burst over the eastern hills. I stretched and yawned and sniffed the morning air. Then I wrinkled my nose in disgust and sneezed! I couldn't smell anything but the flowery shampoo! I rolled vigorously on the dusty ground in hopes it would cover the scent, but it didn't work.

I felt my resolve to stay away from the sewer puddle weakening. Maybe I could quickly roll in the puddle before breakfast. That would be certain to rid me of the horrid shampoo smell. Besides, the cool mud on my furry back would feel good in the already blistering sunshine.

But then I remembered how unhappy I had made my master the day before. I tried to forget about the puddle, but with the smell of that shampoo filling my nostrils, I couldn't think about anything else!

Finally, I just couldn't seem to resist! Although the sun had risen and I was awake, I knew my master was still asleep. It would be easy to quickly sneak to the sewer puddle and be back before he got up.

crept from my doghouse and slunk stealthily away to the sewer puddle. With a hop and a skip and a splash, I buried myself in the muck. In fact, I had so much fun that I forgot about the time. When I finally stopped playing, the sun had risen high in the sky. My stomach growled. Breakfast time had passed long ago.

I hurried home, but my master had already discovered my disappearance. He met me with the hated bathtub filled to the brim with water. And right beside it sat—that's right—a bottle of shampoo!

I knew I had disobeyed. I hung my head in shame and wagged my tail a little bit, hoping I would get some sympathy. I love my master for many things, but most of all because he is patient and forgiving when I am naughty. He gently but firmly placed me in the dreaded tub. Then he began to lather the shampoo into my fur, all the while talking quietly to me.

"Jip, you chose to bring this bath upon yourself. It's not my fault you disobeyed me. Now you have to suffer the consequences. Even though you thought it was fun to roll in the sewer puddle, the results are never enjoyable."

I spent the rest of the day sitting on the front step drying my fur in the hot, afternoon sun ... wishing I had obeyed.

A few days later, I lay gazing at the beautiful sunset. The puffy clouds shone all orange and red in the rays of the sinking sun. Then the sun disappeared, and the clouds darkened into the prettiest purple hues. The moon rose, and the stars appeared and twinkled down at me.

Nighttime in Cambodia is just as hot as in the day, and that night I tossed and turned in my doghouse. I just couldn't sleep. I panted heavily in the stifling humidity.

I had tried my hardest to stay away from the sewer puddle, but I suddenly got a wonderful idea! I could take a cool midnight soak in the sewer puddle! I started out without the slightest thought of my master's words. Well, maybe the thought did try to cross my mind, but I quickly pushed it away.

When I arrived, I found that recent rains had made the sewer puddle more sludgy and inviting than ever. I rolled and wriggled extra hard in it that night—enough to get goop in my ears and all over my face.

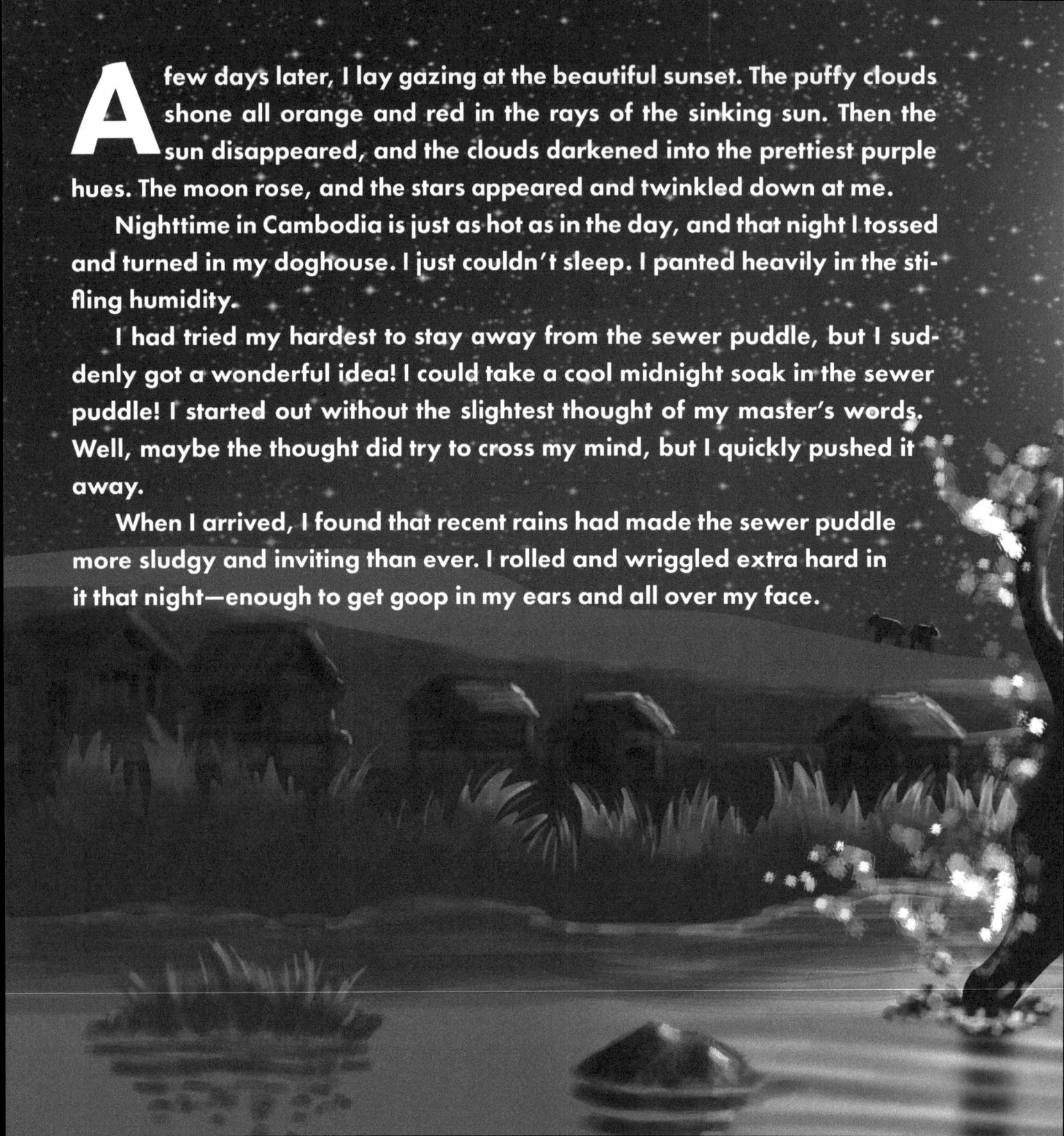

I started home in the moonlight, dripping little drops of goop all the way.

I snuck back into my doghouse and lay down. I knew my master was asleep and had not seen me leave, so maybe he would never know I had disobeyed him and gone to the sewer puddle.

But I had forgotten about how I looked and smelled. The next morning it didn't take my master long to figure out where I had been. I stood before him dripping and smelly and wagging my tail innocently. He immediately brought out the tub, the water, and the shampoo for another awful bath.

I had tried to be an obedient dog and do my master's will, but I gave in instead to what I wanted. My master was right: The consequences that followed my disobedience were the result of my very own choices.

But the flowery smell of shampoo on my coat after the bath was a very small punishment compared to what happened a couple days later.

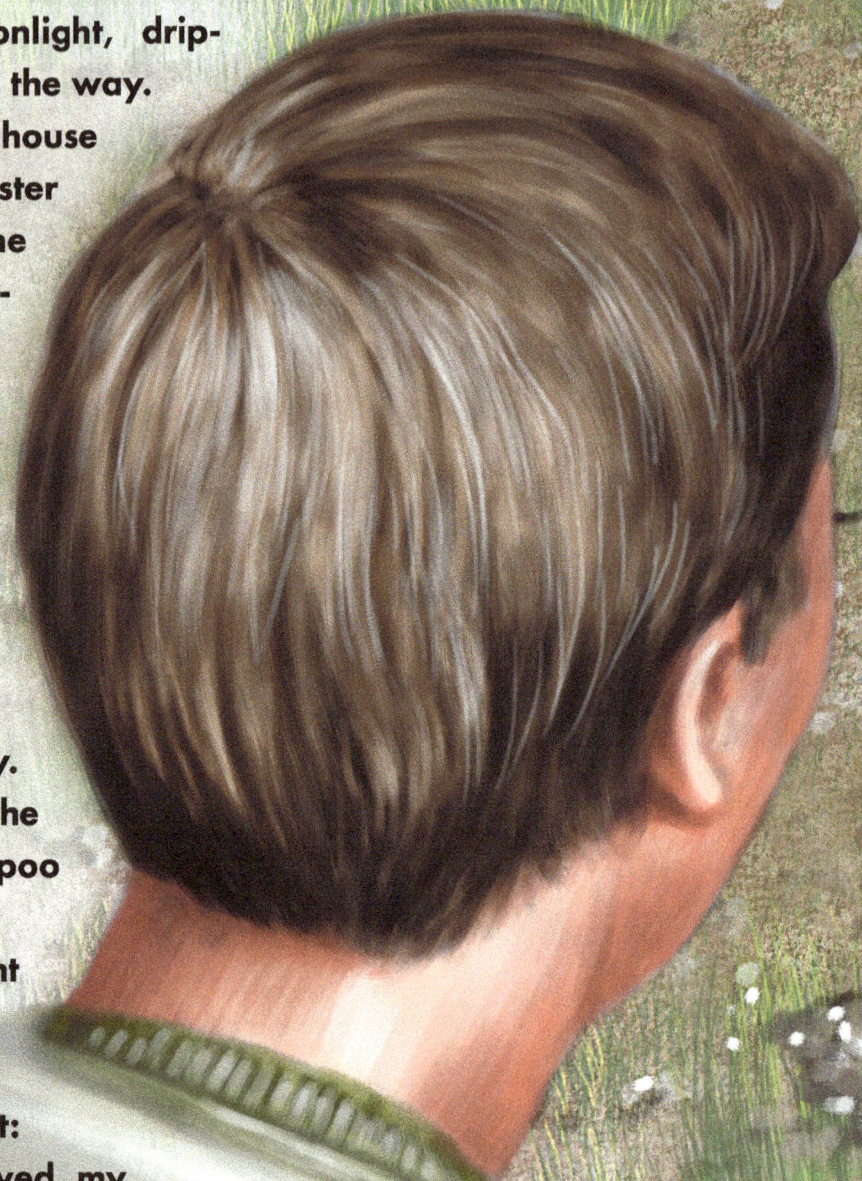

The sun was sinking as I trotted home, dripping with the telltale signs that I had just had a good soak in the sewer puddle. I had again disobeyed my master's command. I tried to push my guilty feelings away, but I just couldn't help feeling unhappy.

Suddenly someone grabbed me from behind and thrust me into a smelly sack! I couldn't see in the darkness, but I got the funny feeling that someone was carrying me somewhere. I struggled, but the top of the sack was tied, and the string wouldn't budge or break. In desperation, I tried to chew a hole in the sack, but that only left a bad taste in my mouth.

I finally lay still, cowering in the bottom of the sack, and a rush of feelings flooded my mind. Did my master know I had disappeared? Would he look for me? If only I hadn't gotten in the habit of going to the puddle! I had been so naughty—my master probably wouldn't even bother to look for me. Why would he want a dog like me anyway? What was going to happen to me?

Suddenly the top of the sack opened, and the person dumped me into a large bin crowded with other dogs. How I wished I had listened to my master! I never realized until that moment what good advice he had. I tried to find a more comfortable position among the packed, squirming bodies, but the other dogs growled and snapped at me!

Then I smelled a smell worse than flowery shampoo, and I suddenly realized what was going to happen to me. The terrible smell of cooked canine stew, which is a delicacy among the natives in Cambodia, filled the air. So death was my punishment! I might have prevented it if I had only listened to my master's command. The minutes seemed like hours, and I began to cry pitifully, although I knew my master couldn't possibly hear me.

Suddenly I heard a step at the door, and then a voice that sounded very familiar spoke to my captor. Could it be? Had my master really come to rescue me? I had to let him know I was there, confined in the awful box. I yelped and jumped, paying no mind to rude nips from the other dogs!

"No, I haven't seen a dog like that anywhere," I heard the dog-catcher deny.

"But, please, just let me look at the dogs you have in that bin," the comforting voice of my master pleaded. Then the heavy lid lifted, and I looked up into the kindest eyes I have ever known. It was my beloved master! He had searched for me and found me!

Then I heard something that almost made my mouth drop open in surprise and disappointment. The awful man who had taken me asked for a large amount of money in exchange for me. The joyful light faded from my eyes, and I groaned and hung my head in despair. I was sure my master would never pay for a naughty pup like me! I knew I wasn't worth it since I hadn't been very faithful or loyal to him.

Yet my master's reassuring voice again shot a ray of hope through the darkness settling over me. "I'll pay whatever you ask—however high the amount is—if I can only take my precious dog back with me!" As I raised my head, I saw my master counting out the money, and my heart soared with love and gratitude.

The price was very high, but my master paid it all, even though it emptied his pocketbook. Soon I was in the security of his loving arms, despite being covered from head to toe with smelly sewer mud. I wiggled and waggled, licking my master again and again to tell him how sorry I was. He forgave me.

My master took me home and brought out the bathtub and shampoo. As he lathered me with soap, he seemed deep in thought. Then he spoke, "Jip, this experience has reminded me of the love of Jesus, who is our heavenly Master."

My master continued, "Before we found you, Jip, you were all alone, wandering the streets and living on garbage. But then we adopted you as our own. In the same way, all of us start our lives in the world's garbage heaps and dark alleys. But Jesus wants to adopt each one of us as His own child. So often we don't want to leave our 'sewer puddle' of naughty sins and habits, even though they bring uncomfortable consequences. Fortunately, Jesus never gives up on us! In fact, the Bible says that He will never leave us or forsake us."

My master rubbed the flowery soap vigorously into my fur, still talking softly. "Our Master, Jesus, does so much for us. Each time we are naughty, He waits patiently for us to come back and ask for forgiveness, and then He washes all the sin away. He says He will never cast away anyone who comes to Him in repentance.

"But no matter how hard we try, we can never leave our 'puddle' of wrongdoings without help. The wages of sin are death, just as you, Jip, faced death in that shack." I shuddered at the memory.

Jesus is the only One who can help us to leave those puddles. He talks to us through His Word, the Bible, and works through parents, teachers, and godly friends. If we listen to them and study God's Word, like you should have listened to me and heeded my words, then we will not go wrong. However, if we continue to stubbornly sneak back to our old habits, Satan will entirely imprison us in the 'bin' of sin! There is still hope, though, isn't there?" My master stroked my back lovingly as he rinsed off the soapsuds.

"Our heavenly Master paid the price of death for us. He gave up everything He had, even His own life, all because He loves us with an everlasting love! When we accept His sacrifice for us, Jesus takes us in His arms just the way we are—our smelly sins and all—and holds us close. Then He cleans up our lives and gives us true victory over our 'sewer puddle' of sins."

My master lifted me from the bathtub and threw out the water in a showering stream. With one last pat, he left me in the warm sunshine to dry.

Needless to say, I never returned to the sewer puddle again. I had learned my lesson! However, that was not the last bath I needed, for we all fail and get our coats dirty at times. But whenever I was tempted to roll in something smelly, I thought of my master. How could I disobey him after he paid such a high price for me? Each time I said "No!" to the temptation, the easier it became to say it again.

In time I even grew to like the smell of the flowery shampoo!

"For God so loved the world that He gave His only begotten Son, that whoever believes in Him should not perish, but have everlasting life" (John 3:16).

We invite you to view the complete
selection of titles we publish at:

www.TEACHServices.com

Scan with your mobile
device to go directly
to our website.

Please write or e-mail us your praises, reactions, or
thoughts about this or any other book we publish at:

TEACH Services, Inc.
P U B L I S H I N G
www.TEACHServices.com ● (800) 367-1844

P.O. Box 954
Ringgold, GA 30736

info@TEACHServices.com

TEACH Services, Inc., titles may be purchased in bulk for
educational, business, fund-raising, or sales promotional use.
For information, please e-mail:

BulkSales@TEACHServices.com

Finally, if you are interested in seeing
your own book in print, please contact us at

publishing@TEACHServices.com

We would be happy to review your manuscript for free.

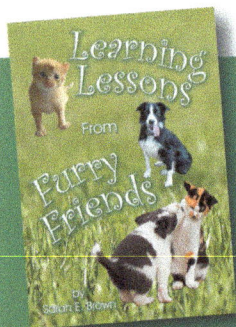

www.ingramcontent.com/pod-product-compliance
Lightning Source LLC
Chambersburg PA
CBHW050357100426
42739CB00015BB/3436